"Alan Hoare is a pastor's pastor: a shepherd's shepherd. As long as I've known him, now nearly forty years, he has devoted himself to biblical reflection, meditation and, like the mystics of long ago, to a yearning after a spirituality that is rooted in 'unchangeable truth'. He is a man of the Word. I am not surprised that he has been drawn to the Psalms. He is a music lover: one who finds peace and rest for the soul in melody and meaning. He has a 'heart after God'. I commend the man. I commend the reading of this devotional pilgrimage."

Rev. Canon Chris Bowater OSL

Chris is considered by many to be a father of the modern worship movement. Coming to prominence in the Charismatic i 1980s, his songs have been translated into n. all over the world.

GW00455121

"Alan Hoare is one of the most devoted stude blessed to know, not just for his learning's sa ... passionate belief in its power to effect godly change in our lives. As a long-time friend and colleague, few men that I've known have so consistently put aside time to 'mine' Scripture for all its worth. The result is a disciple of Christ who can unpeel Scripture in layers, revealing God's imminent presence through His Spirit-breathed Word."

Johnny Markin

Johnny is Emeritus Pastor of Worship Ministries at Northview Community Church, Abbottsford BC, overseeing the development of worship leaders and team training, and leading worship at various venues. He is also seconded to Trinity Western University, where he is an adjunct Instructor in the Worship Arts Department, developing leaders and instructing in worship theology.

"My own spiritual journey benefited enormously from Alan's enthusiastic passion for explaining the Scriptures to me as a friend. I wholeheartedly recommend his daily devotional: bite-sized nuggets of easy-to-understand yet challenging and life-changing theology. Great stuff!"

Andy Piercy

After his conversion, Andy spent three years with Ishmael as a musical duo working as full-time evangelists around the UK. He then spent many years touring and recording as lead singer and songwriter with a professional rock band, 'After The Fire'. Afterwards, he became part of the worship leading team at Holy Trinity Brompton in London from 1993 to 2006. As well as writing and recording many of the songs used on Alpha and at HTB he has also produced records for Delirious, Matt Redman, Soul Survivor and Graham Kendrick. He is now a worship consultant, sharing his deep wisdom with worship teams both here in the UK and in the USA.

"Alan and I have a long history together. We went to school together, played music together, and even went to Bible College together. This being the case, I think I know my old friend pretty well! Alan was always the studious one of the two of us. Whilst I would be reading music magazines, he would be reading Thomas à Kempis. Whilst I would be writing songs, he would be writing Bible studies. And whilst I would be singing to children, he would be sharing theological thoughts with fellow church leaders. So it comes as no surprise that my very learned and godly friend has now put some of his studies into print. With all the research, prayer and time that I know Alan has put into this book, I'm convinced that all who read it will be encouraged, spiritually fed and, most important of all, be brought closer to the God we love and serve. Read, mark, learn and inwardly digest!"

Ishmael

Ishmael is well known for his children's ministry over several decades and has written and recorded over 400 songs (including 'Father God I Wonder') and released around 40 albums of his own and other writers' songs, having produced 15 of these. He has also released 5 music DVDs. Ishmael was ordained into the Anglican Church in 2007 and is now licensed to Chichester Cathedral as their non-stipendiary 'Missioner Deacon' and is affectionately known to the Bishop, Dean and Chapter, and congregation as 'Deacon Ish!'

"Alan's one focus in ministry is God's word. He loves teaching and particularly loves digging into the meaning of words. Alan is eager to find as much as possible in every verse he studies and wants that which he finds to be passed on to as many people as possible. The Song in the Gate is an example of how we begin our week at Alive Church Lincoln. Studying God's word with help from dedicated and informed teachers opens the gate into God's presence. Set a plan to use this material and be blessed."

Stuart Bell

Stuart Bell is the Senior Pastor of Alive Church, a growing multi-site church with several locations in the UK. He also leads the Ground Level Network, a network of around 90 churches and heads up 'Partners for Influence UK', a group of leaders representing influential churches and ministries across the UK. Stuart is actively involved in a number of national leadership forums and is an international speaker and teacher often working into both America and South Africa. Stuart has written four books.

"I first met Alan over forty years ago. We worked closely together for two years on a church planting team in the South of France. His keen questioning spirit coupled with a deep desire to know the Lord impressed me then. The meditations contained in 'The Song in the Gate' demonstrate clearly that his thinking has matured and deepened. The unhurried reading of God's Word has always been, and will always be, the source of effective Christian living. I'm sure that many will be blessed as they read this book."

Chris Short

Chris has a long history of mission. He led teams at Operation Mobilisation in France in the 70's, before becoming the founding pastor of a Baptist church in Pontault-Combault, Paris. Over the years, this church has seen remarkable growth, and now meets in three locations. Since retirement, Chris has visited a number of countries sharing his deep experience of church planting and leadership principles.

"Alan's love of Scripture and his desire to live in the light of the Word is infectious and deeply inspiring. Having sat under Alan's teaching for many years, I can honestly say that his considered study and application of the Word has challenged, inspired and encouraged me on countless occasions. My own personal love of Scripture is down in no small part to the depth and quality of Alan's Bible teaching. As a worship leader I am continually drawn to the great songbook of Scripture and therefore I am thrilled that Alan has drawn together his teachings on the book of Psalms. These comprehensive studies encourage the reader to know in greater depth the beauty of the Psalms and their relevance to the twenty-first century Christian. Alan's writing style is rich yet accessible to all, and I am certain that all who engage in these studies will be developed and discipled into a greater love for God and his Word."

Howard Williams

Over the years, Howard has led several worship teams, has written, recorded and produced worship songs and albums. For many years, he was the worship pastor at the New Life Christian Fellowship (now Alive Lincoln). He now is the executive pastor of Alive church, which meets in several locations. Howard is well known for his musical creativity and skills in directing big musical productions. Howard is married to Clare, one of the pastors at Alive Lincoln.

Onwards and Upwards Publishers

3 Radfords Turf,
Cranbrook,
Exeter,
EX5 7DX
United Kingdom

www.onwardsandupwards.org

First edition (2015) published in the UK by Onwards and Upwards Publishers Ltd.

Second edition (2019) published in the UK by Onwards and Upwards Publishers Ltd.

ISBN: 978-1-78815-534-2
Typeface: Sabon LT
Graphic design: LM Graphic Design / Ben Hoare

PSALM 1

The Song in the Gate

A daily study of the first psalm

Alan Hoare

O&U
Onwards & Upwards

About the Author

Alan was born in Rustington in West Sussex in 1948, and was followed by two younger brothers, Nigel and Simon. His first experience of church ended a few weeks later by him being banned from the local Sunday school for bad behaviour! After leaving school he did an apprenticeship in precision engineering, gaining City and Guilds certificates at Worthing Technical College. It was the 'hippy' era of the 1960s, so weekends were spent with friends, often performing in their rock band, aptly named the 'St James' Infirmary'. A favourite pastime of his is still to pick up his guitar and play the music of that era.

Life changed dramatically for him in March 1969 when he became a Christian as the result of visiting a small Free Church in the little village of Fittleworth, near Petworth. Soon after that, the Baptist Church in Littlehampton became his home church, and also the place where he met Maureen (affectionately known as Mo), who was to become his wife in 1974. Before that, however, they parted company for two years – he to work on a church planting team with Operation Mobilisation in France for two years, and she to do teacher training in Portsmouth.

On returning to England in 1973, Alan studied theology at the Elim Bible College, which was then in Dorking in Surrey, for two years, graduating with a Diploma in Theology. Marriage took place in the middle of the course – highly unusual in those days! This was followed by two years in London, during which time he was an assistant minister at two Elim Pentecostal churches, helped to pioneer two more churches and had two children: Ruth, who was born prematurely in August 1975, and Joseph, who was born in February 1977.

August 1977 saw a move to Lincoln, where he took up the pastorate of an Elim Pentecostal church for nearly ten years. The family meanwhile grew with the added births of Simon in November 1980 and Sarah in March 1982. The family home was an open house, with many visitors staying overnight or for various periods of time.

In Lincoln, Alan quickly developed a strong connection with Stuart Bell, the leader of the large and growing New Life Church there (now

'Alive Church'), and was one of the founder members of the Ground Level network of churches which Stuart started and still leads. In 1987 he joined the New Life Church himself, serving as a member until 1991, when he joined the staff as part of the leadership team. His role was to head up the pastoral and teaching ministry of the church. Benjamin, his youngest son, was born in November that year, completing their family – a biblical quiverful!

In his work for the New Life Church, Alan has also, amongst other things, pastored a number of linked congregations around the area, written and delivered staff devotions, and led marriage preparation, baptismal and membership courses. He is currently teaching 'X-Plore' classes in a number of different churches. Topics covered in this course have included, amongst others, 'The Life and Times of Christ', 'The Life and Times of David', 'The Life of the Apostle Paul', 'Spiritual Theology', 'Systematic Theology' and 'Church History'.

Alan had always dreamt of studying for a degree in theology, and was delighted that the church released him one day a week in 2009 so that he could do this. He attended Mattersey Hall near Doncaster, and was accepted on to the master's course, graduating three years later. For a number of years, he was a contributor for Scripture Union's online WordLive daily devotions.

In 2011, he reduced his time at Lincoln to three days a week, and took on a new role as the senior pastor of a thriving church in Boston, some forty miles east of Lincoln. After three years working for them two days a week, he helped them with the transition to a new senior pastor, and now serves on their leadership team just one day a week as their teaching pastor.

On reaching retirement age in August 2013, Alan retired completely from the staff at Lincoln, and is now able to devote himself more to study, writing and teaching. He has since been teaching in churches both in the Lincolnshire area and abroad. Over the years, he has taught the Scriptures in Mozambique, Vietnam, France, Spain, Poland and Greece. He is currently teaching three different courses in three different churches. Retiring is not in his vocabulary!

Alan feels that his ministry is primarily about building strong and deep spiritual foundations. Strong and mature churches, in his view, are made up of strong and mature believers. He teaches about developing a close and mature walk with Christ, believing that spiritual roots are essential to growing a healthy Christian life. He is passionate about getting people to read the Bible for themselves!

Alan and Mo have now been married for over forty years, and have seen their five children grow up into fine adults. They have, to date, eleven grandchildren!

Alan Hoare can be contacted by email:

alanerichoare@gmail.com

To see all the author's books published by Onwards and Upwards, visit his author page:

www.onwardsandupwards.org/alan-hoare

Or scan the barcode below with your phone:

Preface

At the beginning of 2013, I began to share a little devotional series on the first psalm with the staff and leadership team at my local church. In my opening statements I said:

"For me, these morning meetings are so important. This is the first thing we do at the beginning of our day as a team working here at New Life. And on the first day of our working week, I have the joy of opening up the Scriptures to you, followed by the things that Stuart, our senior pastor, brings to us on Tuesdays; the 'culture Wednesdays' brought by Paul, our executive pastor; the reading aloud of the Scriptures together on a Thursday; and whatever you get up to on a Friday. For my part, these Mondays are specifically geared to ask questions about our personal walk with the Lord, to remind us that our primary concern is not so much what we do for him, but how we are with him, and to keep the focus that our primary purpose and calling is always to walk closely and intimately with Jesus. The work that we do for him must flow out of the walk we have with him. It must take second place. Any work for the kingdom that erodes intimacy and closeness with Christ is, in my view, toxic to the soul. So, at the beginning of the year, for our first staff devotional, I thought it fitting that we should look at the first psalm."

The book was first simply entitled *The First Psalm*, but I subsequently chose to give it the subtitle *The Song in the Gate*. As we approach the gateway to the book, or the field, of Psalms, attentive to the voice of heaven, I believe we will hear this song.

In fact, the whole book of Psalms – or, for the sake of the metaphor, the whole *field* of Psalms – is incredible and vast. They make up the songs, the prayers, and the laments of the people of God over the centuries. They provide a broad landscape of God and his kingdom. Here is where we cut our teeth in praying, as we take upon our lips the prayers of others. Here is where we learn primarily to sing 'the songs of Zion', as we put them to our own music and sing them to the Lord and to each other. As we make our way through them, again and again, praying, singing, weeping, we will become more and more aware of the God who inspired them in the first place. They will bring us to both an intimacy with and a deep, holy respect for the Father, the Son and the Holy Spirit.

Enjoy and experience the journey, but first listen to this first song from the New Living Translation (NLT):

> *Oh, the joys of those who do not follow the advice of the wicked, or stand around with sinners, or join in with mockers.*
>
> *But they delight in the law of the LORD, meditating on it day and night.*
>
> *They are like trees planted along the riverbank, bearing fruit each season.*
>
> *Their leaves never wither, and they prosper in all they do.*
>
> *But not the wicked! They are like worthless chaff, scattered by the wind.*
>
> *They will be condemned at the time of judgment.*
>
> *Sinners will have no place among the godly.*
>
> *For the LORD watches over the path of the godly,*
>
> *But the path of the wicked leads to destruction.*

DAY ONE

Imagine yourself walking into a rather large field in the early and quiet hours of the morning. Through the mist, you see the form of a large tree, standing just beyond the gate. It is there as a welcoming sentinel, ready to greet and inform anyone that chooses to enter the field. It actually beckons to you, inviting you to sit under it for a while to learn of its wisdom. Over several centuries, you see, it has observed human life, and has much to teach. Yet, there is something of God in its origin. Deep in its sap there is a living voice that originated in, and still speaks from, heaven. This tree was planted by an unknown lover of God and his words, but its inspiration and conception came from the Spirit of God. The field is called the book of Psalms. The guardian tree is the first psalm.

The Puritan writer Thomas Watson (1620-1686) wrote:

> *As the book of the Canticles is called the Song of Songs by a Hebraism, it being the most excellent, so this Psalm may not unfitly be entitled, the Psalm of Psalms, for it contains in it the very pith and quintessence of Christianity.*[1]

This particular psalm stands at the entrance to the whole book of psalms, and quite deliberately so, in my view. This book of psalms, containing 150 prayers, laments and songs, is the prayer/song book of both Hebrews and Christians. This is where we learn and cut our teeth in the language of prayer and the expressing of worship. Our praying and our worship need to be firstly schooled in this incredible book. Eugene Peterson strongly points out that if we want to learn to pray, then the best place to start is by using the words and experiences of the psalms. He wrote:

> *Everything that a person can possibly feel, experience, and say is brought into expression before God in the psalms.*[2]

Athanasius of Alexandria (296-373) wrote:

---

[1] Thomas Watson, *The Saint's Spiritual Delight*, (The Religious Tract Company, 1830), p.5

[2] Eugene Peterson, *Answering God – The Psalms as tools for prayer*, (San Francisco, Harper & Row,1989), pp.49,50

11

...the Psalms have a unique place in the Bible because most of the scripture speaks to us, while the Psalms speak for us.[3]

Thought

The book of Psalms is placed roughly in the centre of the Bible. Maybe this is where our attention to Scripture, worship and prayer should be placed in our life as well.

Prayer

Dear God, help me to root out any 'Christian activity' that is actually proving to be toxic to my soul, robbing me of time with you.

---

[3] Athanasius of Alexandria, quoted by Bernard W. Anderson, *Out of the Depths*, (Philadelphia, Westminster Press, 1974)

DAY TWO

Ps.1:1 (ESV)

Blessed is the man who walks not in the counsel of the wicked, nor stands in the way of sinners, nor sits in the seat of scoffers...

The fact that this psalm is located here, right at the beginning, tells me that, at least in God's mind, the Scriptures are important to both our praying and our worship. In fact they are integral and foundational to the whole of our life with God. Our prayers and our worship – indeed, our daily living – must be informed by, rooted in and inspired by the Word of God. It is no coincidence, either, that the longest psalm in the book (Psa.119:1-176) is devoted entirely to the love and a deep receptivity of the Scriptures. This first psalm stands at the gateway to the whole book of Psalms, as if to tell us that the entrance to an authentic life of worship and prayer must start with a love of, and a deep reception of, the Scriptures.

The first verse of the psalm opens with:

> *Blessed is the man who walks not in the counsel of the wicked, nor stands in the way of sinners, nor sits in the seat of scoffers...*

The first word that we encounter is 'blessed'. It is the Hebrew word 'esher', and it is in the plural sense. In other words, the one who is blessed by God is subject to blessing after blessing, pouring out of heaven upon his life. Such is reserved for those who order their lives according to the Scriptures. As we open and delve into its pages, I believe that we open a deep well – a source of heaven's life, heaven's perspectives and heaven's resources. I believe that a life without the Scriptures is misguided, empty of purpose and void of authentic inspiration. When we open the Scriptures, however, we begin to feel the endless succession of heaven's blessings beginning to trickle and flow into our lives.

The opening line is more literally translated, "O the many blessings of that particular man." The plural use of the singular Hebrew word 'esher' denotes not only a *fullness* of blessing, but also a *variety* of blessing. In addition, the word translated 'man' here is 'îysh', and is very emphatic. It means 'that *particular* man'. The man who constructs his life upon the life and Word of God is one in a thousand. The psalmist is saying that such are the manifold blessings upon his life that he stands out from others. He is signally and visibly blessed.

Thought

In our hands is a book that, rightly understood and entered into, will open to us a deep well and usher us into a spiritual landscape that is beautiful beyond words.

Prayer

Father, as I open up the pages of Scripture today, draw me in, and give me a glimpse of the incredibly beautiful kingdom of heaven.

DAY THREE

Ps.1:1 (ESV)

Blessed is the man who walks not in the counsel of the wicked, nor stands in the way of sinners, nor sits in the seat of scoffers...

From my reading of several commentaries, it seems that there are three sets of triplets in this first verse describing the wicked. There is the triplet of the various postures of the wicked: walking, standing and sitting. Then there is the triplet of the character and conduct of the wicked: of their counsel, their way and their seat. Finally, there is the triplet of the degrees of evil in the wicked: the wicked, the sinner and the scoffer.

With the first triplet, we see a change of movement. Sin is progressive and if unchecked, we will find that one thing leads to another. Walking according to ungodly counsel will lead to participating in the lifestyle and walk of ungodly people, which will then bring us to the seat – the place of self-given authority – of the scoffing of the ungodly.

With the second triplet, we see a way of thinking that is alienated and separated from the thinking of God, then a walk that will take us away from the life of God to a self-appointed seat of judgments, opinions and values that end up belittling the ways of God.

With the third triplet we see a distinguishing and a deepening of the depths of depravity in the ungodly. 'The wicked' speaks of those who are uninfluenced by the life and ways of God; 'the sinner' is the one who deliberately adds transgressions to his sin, and 'the scoffer' is the disbeliever who makes a mockery of everything sacred.

In my view, it is much better to be moving slowly and surely into the centre of God's life and counsel than to find ourselves drifting away and becoming desensitised to him because we wouldn't listen to his voice.

Many scholars see this psalm also as the laying down of choices. We can either go the way of the righteous which will lead to a stable and fruitful life, or the way of the wicked which will lead to a fruitless and unstable life. The former is deeply rooted into the life of God, and the latter is blown around by whatever wind that wants to catch it. We need to ask ourselves the question: who and what is influencing us?

Thought

All of us are influenced. It can be by our upbringing, the people around us, the sermons we heard, or the books we read, to name a few. We need, however, to be shaped and influenced by what God says to us through the Scriptures.

Prayer

Dear Lord Jesus, my heart's desire is that as I sit quietly under the Scriptures, taught and mentored by the Holy Spirit, I become influenced and changed from one degree of glory to another, into your likeness.

DAY FOUR

Ps.1:1 (ESV)

Blessed is the man who walks not in the counsel of the wicked, nor stands in the way of sinners, nor sits in the seat of scoffers...

Hudson Taylor (1832-1905) was a missionary to the interior of China for fifty-one years, founding the China Inland Mission. He commented on this "blessed man" in the first line, saying:

...he is happy in what he escapes or avoids, and happy and prospered in what he undertakes.[4]

In other words, as we progress in our spiritual walk, we will find that there is a sharpening of our awareness about what we need to discard and what we need to take up.

Look up Eph.4:20-24; Col.3:5-14; 1.Tim.6:11,12; Heb.12:1,2. In these texts we will read that there are things we need to walk away from and leave behind, and there are things that we need to actively pursue and chase after. Spiritual progress is never made by drifting from one experience to another – it is made by deliberately dealing with and dumping anything that hinders, desensitises, deafens and blinds us to the voice, face and presence of God.

We need to move away from the counsel, the ways and the judgments of the ungodly, however they are expressed, and we need to establish ourselves in the counsel, the ways and the judgments of God. That will involve deep and deliberate choices on our part. Interestingly, Thomas à Kempis wrote:

He to whom the Eternal Word speaks is set free from a multitude of opinions.[5]

This psalm will tell us exactly where to go in order to become accustomed to the thinking and the ways of God. Put very simply, we need to familiarise ourselves with the Scriptures. This will create a framework for life that will hold us together when life threatens to take

---

[4] J. Hudson Taylor, *Blessed Prosperity – Meditations On The First Psalm.* Found in *A Ribband of Blue and Other Bible Studies* (Morgan & Scott, 1899)

[5] Thomas à Kempis, *The Imitation of Christ, Book 1, Chap 3,* translated by George F. Maine, (London, Collins, 1957), p.36

us apart. The Scriptures provide not only a strong foundation for life, but also a strong framework that holds life together. The Scriptures will tell us what God thinks, what God has said, how God works, what God feels, how God reacts. Knowing these things will help us to walk through the ups and downs of life with a deep sense of security. We may not like what is happening to us, but we will know where we are, in whom we live and move and have our being, and in whose hands we reside and rest. Not knowing these things exposes us to insecurities, fears and a walk that is more determined by the feelings of the moment than the facts of divine life.

Thought

According to the text in Heb.12:1, there are things that are sinful, and then there are "weights" (ESV) – "things that hinder" (NIV). These are not sinful in themselves, but they can rob us of spiritual vitality. Can you identify any in your life?

Prayer

Dear Lord, help me to be ruthless in cutting out of my life anything that hinders me from walking close to you, however much it costs.

DAY FIVE

Ps.1:1 (ESV)

Blessed is the man who walks not in the counsel of the wicked, nor stands in the way of sinners, nor sits in the seat of scoffers...

Talking of this "blessed" man, Adam Clark (1760-1832) wrote:

> *His will, desire, affection, every motive in his heart, and every moving principle in his soul, are on the side of God and his truth. He takes up the law of the Lord as the rule of his life...[6]*

This is the testimony of one who has seen the stark difference between what this world has to offer and what is to be found in the counsel and friendship of God. It is therefore suggested that the beauty, the authenticity and the purity of God's thoughts, ways and judgments are by far the better option.

The second verse of the psalm then continues:

> *...but his delight is in the law of the LORD, and on his law he meditates day and night.*

How, then, does the blessed man regard the Scriptures? The psalmist answers by saying that they are a delight to him. This word 'delight' pops up in many places in the Psalms:

- "Great are the works of the LORD, studied by all who delight in them." (Psa.111:4)
- "I will delight in your statutes; I will not forget your word." (Psa.119:16)
- "Your testimonies are my delight; they are my counsellors." (Psa.119:24)
- "Lead me in the path of your commandments, for I delight in it." (Psa.119:35)
- "I find my delight in your commandments, which I love." (Psa.119:47)

---

[6] Adam Clarke, *Commentary on the Bible, vol. 3: Job to Solomon's Song* (Lane & Sandford, 1843)

- "Let your mercy come to me, that I may live; for your law is my delight." (Psa.119:77)
- "If your law had not been my delight, I would have perished in my affliction." (Psa.119:92)

This word 'delight' describes an attitude to the book of God. If we haven't got this attitude of delight, then I strongly suggest that we seek to get it. This will usually start by just getting into the Word of God. As we make a start, we will begin to discover things. As we persevere, we might even just get hooked!

Thought

> *When you delight yourself in the Lord, His Word and His ways become the focus and foundation of your life.*[7]

Prayer

Dear Jesus, please take out of my heart the delights of this world that blind me to the beauty of your face, your words and your kingdom.

---

[7] Elizabeth George, *Loving God with All Your Mind*

DAY SIX

Ps.1:2 (ESV)

...but his delight is in the law of the LORD, and on his law he meditates day and night.

In this psalm, the Scriptures are called the "Law", and it is the Law of God as opposed to the laws of men. Notice the difference: the laws of men are forever changing and being updated. The Law of God, on the other hand, stands eternal, and acts as an immoveable, unchanging measure and bulwark. The Hebrew word is 'tôrâh' (pronounced to-raw), and this word actually has three dimensions to it: law, direction, and instruction. The law shows us the boundaries of life; the direction tells us where to go in life and the instruction tells us how to do life.

The Torah, for the Hebrews, was the first five books of Moses. This was, in fact, the Bible that the psalmist was reading. Eugene Peterson wrote:

...everything that God wanted to say to us was said in Torah. Torah is the basic Bible; everything that follows in Scripture is derivative from it.[8]

Here's a thought: when David prayed in Psa.119:18, "Open my eyes, that I may behold wondrous things out of your law," he wasn't referring to the prophets, the writings, the Gospels or the letters. He, too, was talking about the first five books of Moses. There were wonderful things to be seen there! The Hebrew word for 'wonderful' is pâlâ (pronounced paw-law) and means 'to be marvellous, to be wonderful, to be surpassing, to be extraordinary, distinguished above all else'. A modern translation might be 'mind-blowing'.

Eugene Peterson also taught that the word 'tôrâh' comes from the verb 'yârâh' (pronounced yaw-raw) which means 'to throw' – something like a javelin in order to hit a mark. He writes:

In living speech, words are javelins hurled from one mind to another. The javelin word goes out of one person and pierces another. Not all words are javelin words; some are only tin

---

[8] Eugene Peterson, *Working the Angles – The shape of pastoral integrity*, (Michigan, Eerdmans, 1987), p.54

cans, carrying information from one place to another. But God's word has this aimed, intentional, personal nature. When we are spoken to this way, piercingly and penetratingly, we are not the same. These words get inside us and work their meaning in us.[9]

Thought

The words that we speak to each other can have profound effects. Many of us remember the effects of words spoken at us or into us years ago. God's words are deliberately and intentionally spoken into us to cleanse, heal, restore, challenge and grow us into maturity. We need to open our hearts up to them.

Prayer

Lord, help me this day to open my heart to you, to hear your life-changing words spoken into the depths of my being.

---

[9] Eugene Peterson, *Answering God – The Psalms as Tools for Prayer*, (San Francisco, Harper & Row, 1989), p.25

Day Seven

Ps.1:2 (ESV)

...but his delight is in the law of the LORD, and on his law he meditates day and night.

We approach the Torah not only with delight but also with a deep receptivity. We read not only to learn; we read also to be changed. We do not adapt his word to our way of thinking, our circumstances or even our culture; rather, we allow this word to adapt us to his way of thinking, his large story and the culture of the kingdom of heaven. We read to hear his voice, we read to be drawn into his large story, and we read to develop a deep and profound relationship with him. Just that in itself is designed to be breathtaking. A.W. Tozer wrote:

> *The Bible is not an end in itself, but a means to bring men to an intimate and satisfying knowledge of God, that they may enter into Him, that they may delight in His Presence, may taste and know the inner sweetness of the very God Himself in the core and centre of their hearts.*[10]

Now we come to the getting down to it. Up to this point, it has all been motivational. Delight for the law of God must turn into digging into the law of God. Many profess to love the Bible but have hardly ventured into its pages. Many profess to be Bible-believing Christians but are unaware of what it teaches.

The one who is blessed not only reads and studies the Scriptures, but meditates in them. Let me pause here a little. I have always been struck by the little comment by Robert Cleaver Chapman (1803-1902), who was affectionately known as the 'apostle of love'. He once wrote:

> *...a careless reader of Scripture never made a close walker with God.*[11]

---

[10] A.W. Tozer, *The Pursuit of God*, (Eastbourne, Kingsway Publications, 1982), p.10

[11] R.C. Chapman, *Choice Sayings: Being Notes of Expositions of Scripture*, (London, Morgan & Scott, 1910)

There are three levels of handling the Scriptures here. We read the Scriptures in order to familiarise ourselves with the truth and with the large story of God. We study the Scriptures in order to get under the surface of things. We meditate in the Scriptures in order to get the truth into us.

Thought

> *A Bible that's falling apart usually belongs to someone who isn't.*[12]

Prayer

Holy Father, help me to wipe the dust that has collected on my Bible, and please wipe the dust from the eyes of my heart in order to see the worth of this incredible book you have given to us.

[12] Charles H. Spurgeon

DAY EIGHT

Ps.1:2 (ESV)

...but his delight is in the law of the LORD, and on his law he meditates day and night.

The Hebrew word translated 'meditate' is 'hâgâh', (pronounced haw-gaw), and it literally means, among other things, 'to growl'. Eugene Peterson recalls watching his dog one day gnawing a bone. He wrote:

He gnawed the bone, turned it over and around, licked it, worried it. Sometimes we could hear a low rumble or growl, what in a cat would be a purr.[13]

Meditation in the Scriptures, according to Peterson, is a "dog-with-a-bone kind of reading".[14] Some writers have likened it to "chewing the cud"; others, like Charles Bridges (1794-1869), call the practice of meditation "the digestive faculty of the soul"[15]. Stephen Binz, a Roman Catholic scholar, spoke of it as "letting the Scriptures take root in us, penetrating the deepest part of our being so that they become part of us."[16] Jim Packer wrote:

Meditation is the activity of calling to mind, and thinking over, and dwelling on, and applying to oneself, the various things that one knows about the works and ways and purposes and promises of God, by the help of God, as a means of communion with God. Its purpose is to clear one's mental and spiritual vision of God, and to let His truth make its full and proper impact on one's heart and mind.[17]

We need to state two things at this point. Firstly, this is a meditating *in the Scriptures*. Other forms of meditation will ask us to empty our

---

[13] Eugene Peterson, *Eat this Book – the Art of Spiritual Reading*, (London, Hodder & Stoughton, 1987), p.1

[14] Ibid, p.4

[15] Charles Bridges, *Psalm 119 – an exposition*, (Edinburgh, Banner of Truth, 1977), p.31

[16] S.J Binz, *Conversing with God in Scripture*, (Maryland, The Word among us Press, 2008), p.61

[17] James. I. Packer, *Knowing God*, (London, Hodder & Stoughton, 1973), p.20

minds; biblical meditation, on the other hand, encourages us to fill, not only our minds, but our hearts with Scripture. In this way, the Scriptures become part of us – the word becomes flesh, if you like.

Secondly, this discipline cannot be performed in a climate of rush and noise. Sadly, this is the atmosphere in which many of us live and breathe, and so life is fast and furious, producing many exciting experiences but few life-changing encounters. An 'in depth' encounter with God in his Word insists that we must stop. The poet William Henry Davies (1871-1940) wrote:

> *...what is this life if full of care – we have no time to stand and stare?*[18]

We must learn to chew long and lovingly on this Word.

Thought

Guigo II was a Carthusian monk and the 9th prior of the Grande Chartreuse monastery in the French Alps from 1174-80. He wrote:

> *...reading puts as it were whole food into your mouth; meditation chews it and breaks it down...*

Prayer

Dear Lord, deliver me from spiritual snacking.

---

[18] W.H. Davies, *Leisure*, retrieved from
   http://www.davidpbrown.co.uk/poetry/william-henry-davies.html

DAY NINE

Ps.1:2 (ESV)

...but his delight is in the law of the LORD, and on his law he meditates day and night.

Thomas à Kempis wrote:

> *In silence and quietness the devout soul makes progress and learns the hidden mysteries of the Scriptures.*[19]

God spoke to Isaiah the prophet, talking of a lion growling over his prey. (Isa.31:4) This is this same Hebrew word 'hâgâh', often translated 'meditating'. The lion was lost in his gnawing, oblivious to the hunters who were surrounding him. We, too, can become so absorbed in our enjoyment of the Word of God that our immediate surroundings take second place in our thinking. Meditation in the Scriptures was meant to be 'ruminative and leisurely'. Our meditation is not out of duty, but out of pure delight.

Another little phrase that catches our attention is 'night and day'. This is just an expression meaning 'all the time' or 'continually'. In other words, we are constantly at it – like a dog with a favourite bone. Again and again, we will return to it, seeking to extract more goodness out of it. For us, the Bible becomes not just a book that is brought out on a weekly basis to accompany us to church; rather, it becomes a familiar friend – communed with on a daily basis. It becomes a loved and cherished companion, who speaks to us of the things and ways of God. The opening of its pages brings the reader face to face with God and within range of his voice. He anticipates the opening of its pages.

Years ago, I read the story of Robert Murray M'Cheyne (21st May 1813 - 25th March 1843). He was a Scottish Presbyterian minister in Dundee, who died prematurely of typhus. He would rise early in the morning each day to spend time with the Lord. In his personal journal is this moving entry:

---

[19] Thomas à Kempis, *The Imitation of Christ*, Book 1, chap 20, translated by Leo Sherley-Price, (London, Penguin, 1952), p.51

February 23rd – Sabbath – Rose early to seek God, and found Him whom my soul loves. Who would not rise early to meet such company? [20]

Thought

Maybe we ought to think about getting some 'duvet victories' – where we are able to crawl out from underneath our duvets in the morning to seek the company of the one who deeply loves us, and desires to meet with us, in the quietness of the dawn.

Prayer

Dear Lord, help me to respond to you when you touch my spirit in my waking hours.

---

[20] Andrew Bonar, *Robert Murray M'Cheyne*, (Edinburgh, Banner of Truth Trust, 1972), p.30

DAY TEN

Ps.1:2 (ESV)

...but his delight is in the law of the LORD, and on his law he meditates day and night.

Thinking of our studying, meditating, pondering or musing in the Scriptures, Charles Bridges cites some advice given to a group of young ministers. The teacher said:

Study close; especially make the Bible your study. There is no knowledge, which I am more desirous to increase in, than that. Men get wisdom by books; but wisdom towards God is to be gotten out of God's book; and that by digging. Most men do but walk over the surface of it, and pick up here and there a flower. Few dig into it. Read other books to help you understand that book. Fetch your prayers and your sermons from thence. The volume of inspiration is a full fountain, ever overflowing, and hath always something new.[21]

We need to capture the spirit of yearning that is manifested here. The sons of Korah wrote:

As the deer longs for streams of water, so I long for you, O God. I thirst for God, the living God.[22]

King David wrote:

O God, You are my God; I earnestly search for you. My soul thirsts for you; my whole body longs for you in this parched and weary land where there is no water. I have seen you in your sanctuary and gazed upon your power and glory.[23]

The words that are used here are reminiscent of other words such as 'pining' and 'aching'.

Through the pages of Scripture, the psalmist encountered God, and he was ushered into vistas of unspeakable beauty and dimension. He lost track of the world around him for a time. God filled his vision.

---

[21] Footnote 1, Cited by Charles Bridges, *The Christian ministry*, (Banner of Truth, Edinburgh, 1830), p.51

[22] Psa.42:1,2

[23] Psa.63:1,2

Hopefully by now, we are getting to grips with the importance of giving serious attention to the Scriptures. This will involve making it a priority in our busy schedules. For me personally, apart from the voices of my family at home, the first voice that I really want to hear in the morning is that of the Lord. My phone, my diary and my social networking systems all take a very low second place to his voice. After having heard him, I feel that I am ready to hear the voices of others.

Thought

There was an ache in the soul of David. It could only be assuaged by the presence of God. Meditating in the Scriptures and subsequent worship took him there.

Prayer

Dear Father, I find too many desires rising up within me, all clamouring for my attention. Help me to silence those that distract me and drag me down, and to give room for that deeper desire to touch your face.

DAY ELEVEN

Ps.1:3a (ESV)

He is like a tree planted by streams of water...

The psalmist now plunges us into a powerful metaphor of a tree. This image is used often in the Scriptures for many different reasons. The blessed man, the one who gives himself to the Word of God shall be "like a tree". My immediate thoughts are that of strength and stability. During my missionary years in Southern France in the early 70s, we would travel about fifteen miles each day from the small village of Courthézon to the larger town of Bolléne, where we were endeavouring to plant a church. For much of the journey, the route was flanked by trees. On a regular basis, we would sadly see cars that had veered off the road for one reason or another, and had wrapped themselves around these trees. In almost all cases, the accident had resulted in fatalities. Such was the strength of the trees that they had withstood whatever was thrown at them.

In Psa.119:165 we read these words:

> *Great peace have they that love Thy law, nothing shall make them stumble.*

The peace they enjoy is noted for its abundance. Whatever life hurls at them, they are somehow kept in an abundance of peace. Saturation in the Scriptures results in a deep-seated saturation of peace, and a deep security of heart and mind. As noted before, the Scriptures provide not only a strong foundation for life, but also a strong framework that holds life together.

My thinking is that the people who are 'tree-like' are deeply rooted people. The landscapes of life may change around us, but those who are deeply rooted in God and his Word become 'reference points' in the life of the church and even the communities in which they live. Large, well-established trees provide shade from the heat and they also provide shelter for the vulnerable. Using other metaphors, Isaiah said of godly leaders:

...each will be like a hiding place from the wind, a shelter from the storm, like streams of water in a dry place, like the shade of a great rock in a weary land.[24]

When the hurricanes of life show up, we will either be blown down and away, or we will bend with it and remain standing. What's your preference?

Thought

There is no such thing as a spiritual journey. If a little shocking, this is refreshing. If there were a spiritual journey, it would be only a quarter-inch long, though many miles deep.[25]

We are usually more concerned about the visibility of our ministry whereas God is more concerned with the depth of our ministry.

Prayer

Dear Jesus, help me not to be skin deep in my walk with you, but help me to put some depth into it.

---

[24] Isa.32:1,2
[25] Meister Eckhart

32

DAY TWELVE

Ps.1:3a (ESV)

He is like a tree planted by streams of water…

I believe that God wants us to be people of strength and stability – strong reference points in the storms and vicissitudes of life, exercising a restful poise of faith and trust. To the question, "Where does faith come from?" the answer will always be, "Faith comes by hearing, and hearing by the word of Christ." (Rom.10:17)

We now look at the location of this tree. It is "planted by streams of water". The way the Hebrew language is arranged here strongly suggests that it is not a spontaneous or random planting, but a deliberate and a well thought through action that is determined to offer the sapling the best resources possible. At this point my mind goes to Psa.92:12,13, where it is written:

> *The righteous flourish like the palm tree and grow like a cedar*
> *in Lebanon. They are planted in the house of the LORD; they*
> *flourish in the courts of our God.*

The word 'planted' found in both Psa.1:3 and Psa.92:13 is the Hebrew word 'shâthal' (pronounced shaw-thal), and it carries not only the meaning of 'planted' but more so of being 'transplanted'. This is wonderful, because our lives are testimonies of being transplanted from the dominion of this world into the good soil of the kingdom of heaven. The apostle Paul put it this way:

> *He has delivered us from the domain of darkness and*
> *transferred us to the kingdom of his beloved Son…*[26]

Our roots have been tenderly lifted out of the soil of darkness and placed just as tenderly into the good soil of the kingdom of heaven. New life now begins to course through us, effecting changes, healing and cleansing moral and spiritual diseases, empowering and envisioning us.

The 'streams of water' are better translated 'deliberately cut out canals', once again giving the idea of purposeful planning. God sees to it that we are set into good and resourcing places that have been specifically designed to nourish our spiritual lives. It is my firm conviction, according

---

[26] Col.1:13

to the psalm we quoted above, that the primary place of the nourishment of the soul is to be found in the setting of the local church. My walk with Christ is first nourished, of course, by my private and secret walk with the Lord in his Word, but it is also strengthened, shaped and authenticated by my walk with fellow believers. In fact, they are both integral to an authentic walk with God. One without the other is lopsided. The river of God runs through the church, and God will want to transplant us into one of his local expressions of church.

Thought

Our local church, although not perfect, is the very place where God wants to nurture us. Our brothers and sisters in the faith have been strategically placed to walk with us, the light of Christ shining through their weaknesses and imperfections.

Prayer

Thank you, Lord, for where you have placed me. Help me to participate in the giving and receiving of your life among the people in my church.

DAY THIRTEEN

Ps.1:3b (ESV)

...that yields its fruit in its season...

I love walking in forests. They give me a sense of history, and they also give me a sense of the random beauty of God's creation. I have, however, never seen a fruit tree in a forest. There is an interesting comment, though, by the girl in the Song of Solomon when she describes her beloved. She says:

> *As an apple tree among the trees of the forest, so is my beloved among the young men. With great delight I sat in his shadow, and his fruit was sweet to my taste.*[27]

Out of all the trees in the forest, he was the only one who bore fruit. Out of all relationships to be had in this life, our relationship with Christ is the most fruitful.

Some trees are simply for decoration – they make a garden or a landscape look beautiful. In the first garden, the Garden of Eden, there were two kinds of trees. There were those that were "pleasing to the sight" and then there were those that were "good for food". In this garden, God walked and spoke with the first couple. I love this comment by Watchman Nee:

> *The garden is for beauty and pleasure. There are trees, but not for timber; there is fruit, but not for commercial produce.*[28]

Our walking with Christ in the garden of our soul is never to be commercialised, but enjoyed and wondered at. Sometimes, he will share things with us that can be communicated to others, but also he will want to have secrets with us. We are wise when we discern between the two. Lovers do not go public on everything.

Here in this psalm we have a fruit-bearing tree. A fruit-bearing tree exists for the benefit of others. Unpicked fruit rots and drops. The fruit we produce is designed to feed and nourish others. Our walk with Christ takes priority over all other relationships, but it must never become

---

[27] Song.2:3
[28] Watchman Nee, *The Song of Songs*, translated by Elizabeth K. Mei and Daniel Smith, (Alresford, CLC, 1965), p.107

purely for our own pleasure and benefit. Spiritual narcissism rots the soul. What we receive from the Lord, we must pass on. Like Abraham, we are blessed in order to become a blessing. Even the best monastics are agreed on this: true and authentic contemplation results in mission to the world. And didn't Mother Theresa do it well!

Thought

If you sit long enough in the presence of Christ, you will feel his heartbeat. It will not only be for you; it will also be for those who have never known him.

Prayer

Dear Jesus, may our times together in the quietness produce much fruit that others can partake of.

DAY FOURTEEN

Ps.1:3b (ESV)

…that yields its fruit in its season…

L et us consider further the fruit-bearing tree. Its fruit, emerging from our silent and slow meditation in the Word of God, comes "in its season". In other words, it is neither advanced nor retarded. It comes on time. I remember watching a Billy Graham film in France back in the early 70s. Although it was done through French translation, I could just about pick up the spoken English as I stood next to the loudspeaker. I remember being struck by the spiritual authority of the man, and prayed this prayer: "Lord, what you took twenty years to produce in him, please do it in me in two." I think I heard God chuckle.

We need not stress ourselves at the slowness of God. Overstimulating the things and the workings of God usually ends up badly. If we concentrate on feeding from the Word, he will concentrate on the development of fruit in us. We eat – he makes us grow.

Pushing the work of God is never productive. In my experience, if ever I feel that I have to push God, I have also found that he digs his heels in. Fruit comes when it is ready. Jesus, talking about the growth of the kingdom, said that after sowing the seed "the earth produces by itself, first the blade, then the ear, then the full grain in the ear". (Mk.4:28) I want pick up on the phrase "by itself". The Greek word is 'automatos'. It does it by itself – automatically. It does not grow any quicker by constant examining and prodding by the farmer. The same phrase is used by Jesus in a different sense. He said:

> *Abide in me, and I in you. As the branch cannot bear fruit by itself, unless it abides in the vine, neither can you, unless you abide in me.*[29]

In this sense then, the fruit comes, not from the branch's endeavours, but by its simple abiding in the vine. The fruitfulness that God looks for in us does not come from any natural ability that we might have in ourselves, but from loving and intimate communion with Christ himself. The message is clear: stop striving; get intimate with him and start feeding. The fruit will emerge.

---

[29] John.15:4

We are in such a hurry. I once read a powerful little book called 'The Sounds of God' by Michael Mitton. He concluded:

> ...if we are to hear God, then we will need to make space and spend time in sanctified sauntering, rather than becoming obsessed with the finishing post.[30]

I like that word 'sauntering'. I think Michael Mitton has a lot to teach us.

Thought

God is not in a hurry. It is not in his nature, and neither should it be in ours.

Prayer

Dear God, please take the hurry and striving out of my soul, and help me to appreciate sauntering and exploring with you.

---

[30] Michael Mitton, *The Sounds of God*, (Wiltshire, Eagle, 1993), p.76

DAY FIFTEEN

Ps.1:3c (ESV)

...and its leaf does not wither...

There is a withering that comes with death, and that happens to all of us. Here, however, I believe that the psalmist is talking about a premature withering – a withering that should not be happening. The psalmist is pondering a deeply rooted tree which does not have withering leaves in the summer. The life of God, drawn up through deep roots in the Scriptures, sustains the leaves against the heat of the sun. This is the message here. The leaves remain hydrated and moist under heat.

My mind goes to the parable of the sower, where the seed that doesn't take deep root actually withers under the heat of trials, tribulations and pressures. Jesus said:

> *Other seed fell on rocky ground, where it did not have much soil, and immediately it sprang up, since it had no depth of soil. And when the sun rose, it was scorched, and since it had no root, it withered away.*[31]

God doesn't want us to be 'flash-in-the-pan' Christians. He desires instead that we become people who are fully hydrated and moist, nourished by the life of God, in whatever heat we find ourselves coming under. Fruit and fidelity all emerge out of sinking our roots deep into the good soil of the Scriptures.

Twelve times in the Old Testament, and eight times in the psalms, we come across the little phrase "in the day of trouble" or the "day of distress". Two Hebrew words are used. The first one, translated 'trouble' is 'tsâr' (pronounced tsaw) and its root word 'tsârâr' (pronounced tsaw-raw). This word denotes difficulties that put us under extreme and painful pressure. Words like 'cramped', 'squeezed', 'squashed', even 'crushed' come to mind. The other word is 'ra' (pronounced rah) and it simply means 'evil' or 'bad'.

There are days when things goes wrong, when we find ourselves hurting under real pressures that seek to restrict us, hamper us and even stop us in our tracks. Sometimes it comes from adverse circumstances,

---

[31] Mk.4:5,6

and sometimes it come from difficult people. Sometimes it comes at such a pace and strength that humanly speaking you feel that you are not going to cope with it. And then there is the bad and evil stuff. Please remember that being a frontline Christian puts you, not only under pressure, but also in the firing line. Evil is often personified, and seeks to hinder us, harm us and even destroy us.

Thought

Someone once said that "we need to learn how to turn stumbling blocks into stepping stones".

Prayer

Dear Lord, teach me how to respond well, not react badly to adverse conditions.

DAY SIXTEEN

Ps.1:3c (ESV)

...and its leaf does not wither...

Why are we surprised when things happen, and especially when things goes wrong or we get hammered? Peter, in his first letter, wrote:

Beloved, do not be surprised at the fiery trial when it comes upon you to test you, as though something strange were happening to you...[32]

The New Testament writers agree in saying something like, "Get used to it – this is the job lot of the followers of Christ." James, in his letter, said:

Count it all joy, my brothers, when you meet trials of various kinds, for you know that the testing of your faith produces steadfastness. And let steadfastness have its full effect, that you may be perfect and complete, lacking in nothing.[33]

J.B. Phillips (PHI) put it this way:

When all kinds of trial and temptations crowd into your lives, my brothers, don't resent them as intruders, but welcome them as friends! Realise that they come to test your faith and to produce in you the quality of endurance.

Eugene Peterson puts it yet another way in the Message (MSG):

Consider it a sheer gift, friends, when tests and challenges come at you from all sides. You know that under pressure, your faith-life is forced into the open and shows its true colours.

You see, God has this incredible knack of using pressures and trials in order to strengthen and refine us, and to strengthen and refine our faith. Whatever our theology is, we will find that most pressures and difficulties are specifically designed for our growth. Always, always, the key is how we respond to it. Our attitude is everything.

---

[32] 1.Pet.4:12
[33] Jas.1:2,3

Charles Swindoll wrote:

The longer I live, the more I realise the impact of attitude on life. Attitude, to me, is more important than facts. It is more important than the past, than education, than money, than circumstances, than failures, than successes, than what other people say or do. It is more important than appearance, giftedness or skill. It will make or break a company, a church, a home. The remarkable thing is that we have a choice every day regarding the attitude we will embrace for that day. We cannot change our past, we cannot change the fact that people will act in a certain way. We cannot change the inevitable. The only thing we can do is to play on the one string we have, and that is our attitude. I am convinced that life is 10% what happens to me and 90% how I react to it. And so it is with you and I; we are in charge of our attitudes.[34]

Thought

Am I in charge of my attitudes, or are they in charge of me?

Prayer

Dear Lord, help me this day to choose the right attitude to whatever comes my way.

---

[34] Charles Swindoll, *Attitude*, retrieved from
http://www.goodreads.com/quotes/267482-the-longer-i-live-the-more-i-realize-the-impact

DAY SEVENTEEN

Ps.1:3d (ESV)

In all that he does, he prospers.

Up to this point, we have been looking at the quality of this tree. It is mature and stable, well rooted within easy reach of the nourishment of God, bearing fruit easily and without external pressure, and it is not withering under the heat. All this comes from giving serious attention to the reading of, and meditation in, the Scriptures.

Now we come to the visible fruit of all this loving time and labour in the Scriptures: "In all that he does, he prospers." That is a huge statement, and it is not the only time it is mentioned. In Josh.1:8, it reads:

> *This Book of the Law shall not depart from your mouth, but you shall meditate on it day and night, so that you may be careful to do according to all that is written in it. For then you will make your way prosperous, and then you will have good success.*

King David, as he lay dying said to Solomon, his son:

> *Keep the charge of the LORD your God, walking in his ways and keeping his statutes, his commandments, his rules, and his testimonies, as it is written in the Law of Moses, that you may prosper in all that you do and wherever you turn...[35]*

Finally, James wrote:

> *The one who looks into the perfect law, the law of liberty, and perseveres, being no hearer who forgets but a doer who acts, he will be blessed in his doing.[36]*

Meditating in, and practising, the truths of the Scriptures – these are the keys to a spiritual prosperity that outworks itself into a richness of soul and a success in all our doing. The word that the psalmist uses is 'tsâlach' (pronounced tsaw-lakh). According to Strong's Hebrew Dictionary, the word means 'to push forward or to break out'.[37] The

---

[35] 1.Kgs.2:3
[36] Jas.1:25
[37] James Strong, *Hebrew Dictionary of the Bible*, e-sword.net

Brown-Driver-Briggs Hebrew Dictionary adds, 'to advance, to prosper, to make progress, to succeed, to be profitable.'[38] The Keil and Delitzsch Commentary on the Old Testament notes of this man that "everything he takes in hand he brings to a successful issue".[39]

Thought

Of all the kinds of prosperity there are out there, what kind are you looking for?

Prayer

Dear God, please fill my heart and soul with a divine prosperity that will enrich the lives of those around me.

---

[38] Brown-Driver-Briggs, *Hebrew Dictionary*, e-sword.net
[39] Keil and Delitzsch, *Commentary on the Old Testament*, e-sword.net

DAY EIGHTEEN

Ps.1:3d-4 (ESV)

In all that he does, he prospers. The wicked are not so, but are like chaff that the wind drives away.

The blessed individuals whom we considered yesterday are not just visionaries who see things and starts things; they are also completers of things. There is a strong sense of the manifold blessings of God on everything to which they put their hands to. Moses prayed:

Let the favour of the Lord our God be upon us, and establish the work of our hands upon us; yes, establish the work of our hands! [40]

The Hebrew word translated 'establish' means 'to be firm, to be stable, to be established'. The quality and calibre of their work reflects the quality and calibre of their life. As Dr Leupold says:

...it will be obvious in such a life that God is crowning the man's endeavours with success. Tokens of Divine favour abound. [41]

I feel that this is very much worth investing in and working towards. Success, gotten God's way, has longevity and sustainability built into it. Perseverance in the Scriptures will bring a deep level of the favour of God upon the works of our hands.

When we talk about God prospering those who take seriously the Scriptures, it is not a reward. Rather it is the result of living closely with God and his word.

Peter Craigie wrote:

Just as a tree with a constant water supply naturally flourishes, so too the person who avoids evil and delights in Torah naturally prospers. [42]

---

[40] Psa.90:17
[41] H.C. Leupold, *Exposition of Psalms*, (London, Evangelical Press, 1969), p.36
[42] Peter Craigie, *Word Biblical Commentary on the Psalms, Vol. 1*, (Waco, Texas, Word Books, 1983), p.61

Verse four says:

The wicked are not so, but are like chaff that the wind drives away...

We now come face to face with the wicked and their fate. We will see that the outcome of their lives is set in stark contradistinction against that of the blessed man. Dr Leupold writes:

We might think of the course of the wicked as a path that becomes increasingly less clearly defined and finally loses itself in a swamp and morass.[43]

The Hebrew word is 'râshâ' (pronounced 'raw-shaw'). Keil and Delitzsch, writing in 1866, wrote that the word meant 'the godless, whose moral condition is lax, devoid of stay, and as it were gone beyond the reasonable bounds of true unity...'[44] In other words, these were people without God in their lives – with no strong definitive morals, no perseverance at anything, and no ability to foster genuine community. I think that this accurately describes the postmodern culture in which we live in today. You see, nothing really changes...

Thought

The wisdom and ways of God are ageless and have no need to be adapted to modern cultural tastes.

Prayer

Dear Lord, please put a strong, unfluctuating moral consistency into my life.

---

[43] H.C. Leupold, *Exposition of Psalms*, (London, Evangelical Press, 1969), p.38

[44] Keil and Delitzsch, *Commentary on the Old Testament*, e-sword.net

DAY NINETEEN

Ps.1:4 (ESV)

The wicked are not so, but are like chaff that the wind drives away.

L et us linger with the wicked a little longer. The commentators Kiel and Delitzsch go on to describe these people as…

…without root below, without fruit above, devoid of all the vigour and freshness of life, lying loose upon the threshing-floor and a prey of the slightest breeze – thus utterly worthless and unstable.[45]

The psalmist further describes them as "chaff". Chaff is the protective husk that surrounds the grain. After a harvest, both grain and husk are thrown into the air – the grain returns to the ground and the husk is blown away. Here's a thought: flying high in the purposes of God will both reveal that which is true and authentic, and remove the chaff from our lives. It will sift those who are authentic and substantial from those who are mere pretenders.

Chaff also makes the grain look larger than it actually is. That is another reason why we are, at times, sifted – thrown into a sieve and thrown hard into the air. The whole process is to reduce us down to our actual size. Peter's denial of Jesus was, in essence, a sifting. He had promised much with his mouth, but when the moment came, he actually bottled out. A careful reading of Lk.22:31-34 and Jn.21:15-19 will demonstrate that Peter actually came to realise that his declared love for Jesus wasn't at the same level as his actual love for Jesus.

Chaff is no match for a well-rooted tree. In a storm, the tree may bend, but the chaff will disappear. The storms of life will separate the true from the false, and those who are authentic from those who are shallow pretenders – the rooted from the rootless.

This little 'Song of the Gate' says that the wicked are chaff-like – in other words, they are of little or no substance, and they are driven away by the wind. The word translated 'drives' is 'nâdaph' (pronounced naw-daf), and means literally 'to shove apart, to disperse'. It is a forceful word.

---

[45] Keil and Delitzsch, *Commentary on the Old Testament*, e-sword.net

Thought

When the storms of life hit us, will we stand firmly rooted in Christ, or will we be blown away?

Prayer

Dear Lord, may I submit to the loving but firm sieving of my faith, knowing that you are intent in revealing who I really am.

DAY TWENTY

Ps.1:5 (NLT)

They will be condemned at the time of judgment. Sinners will have no place among the godly.

The preacher C.H. Spurgeon once talked about "the vehement tempest of death, which sweeps away the soul of the ungodly"[46]. Let me put it firmly in this way: death will come to us all. We are still under the judgment of death given to Adam, our forefather – it has not been rescinded. Its power has been broken by the death and resurrection of Christ, but it is not rescinded. It still comes. In fact it is the last enemy to be put under the feet of the Saviour. Looking into the future, Paul wrote:

The last enemy to be destroyed is death.[47]

When it does come to us, however, I believe that for those who have trusted in Christ it will be a gentle calling into the presence of the Lord. For the unbeliever, on the other hand, it will be a frightening and terrifying thrusting and shoving, against their will, into an eternal and horrifying destination.

I remember watching a film one night – a typical thriller, and yet the death scenes of the villains were quite remarkable, in what I felt were the most accurate depictions of godless deaths I have ever seen. In one such scene, the pursued criminal ran across a road and was hit by a fast moving car. Death was instantaneous. As I continued to watch, the man's soul seemed to rise up from within himself, and for a few seconds he stood there looking at his body in shock and disbelief. Then all of a sudden, out of seeming nowhere came seven or eight dark shadowy figures, who then firmly took hold of him and with the speed of a train, dragged him away into the darkness. You could hear him screaming into the distance.

This is one reason why the mission of God – the preaching of the gospel – is so important for us. If the enemy of our souls can convince us that an eternal hell is not a reality, then the mission of the church loses

---

[46] Charles Spurgeon, C.H., *Treasury of David, Vol.1,* (London, Marshall Brothers), p.8
[47] 1.Cor. 15:26

much, if not all, of its impetus. We need to take to heart the words of C.T. Studd:

> *Some wish to live within the sound of church or chapel bell; I want to run a rescue shop within a yard of hell.*[48]

The apostle Paul wrote of his inner compulsion from the Lord to preach the gospel:

> *For if I preach the gospel, that gives me no ground for boasting. For necessity is laid upon me. Woe to me if I do not preach the gospel!* [49]

Thought

If people need to be saved, should that affect the reason and the way we do evangelism? Do we have a responsibility? (Check out Ez.33:1-9/Acts 18:6; 20:26,27.)

Prayer

Dear God, please help me to see the lost as you see them, and may my heart be moved with an urgent compassion for them.

---

[48] Norman Grubb, *C.T. Studd, Cricketer and Pioneer*, (Lutterworth Press, London, 1939), p.166
[49] 1.Cor.9:16

DAY TWENTY-ONE

Ps.1:5 (NLT)

*They will be condemned at the time of judgment. Sinners will have
no place among the godly.*

There is a day of judgment that is coming. We are foolish if we
ignore this fact, or if we do not let it affect the way we do life here
on earth. The thoughts of eternity need to shape and inform our
thinking and planning.

This fifth verse of the song emphasises this point clearly. The English
word 'stand' is the Hebrew word 'qûm' (pronounced koom), and it
literally means 'to rise'. Albert Barnes wrote:

> *The idea is that they will not be found among those who are
> acquitted by the Judge, and approved by him. The idea seems
> to be derived from the act of standing up to be tried, or to
> receive a sentence.*[50]

Derek Kidner puts it this way:

> *…before the Judge they will have, in our similar phrase, not a
> leg to stand on, and among his people no place.*[51]

Writing in the context of there being both 'genuine' and 'pretend'
Christians within church circles, Matthew Henry quoted the Chaldean
and Aramaic, saying:

> *…that great day will be a day of discovery, a day of
> distinction, and a day of final division.*[52]

Here we have the tough realities of the final consequences of the
choices that we make in life. And it all hinges on whom we choose to
listen to. We can either heed the alluring and conflicting voices of the
ungodly, or we can take note of the clear and definitive Word of God.
Jesus himself talked of two gates that led to two different ways. He said:

---

[50] Albert Barnes, *Notes on the Bible*, e-sword.net
[51] Derek Kidner, *Psalms 1-72*, (Leicester, IVP, 1973), p.49
[52] Matthew Henry, *Henry's Commentary, Vol.2*, (London, Partridge &
Oakley, 1849), p.105

Enter by the narrow gate. For the gate is wide and the way is easy that leads to destruction, and those who enter by it are many. For the gate is narrow and the way is hard that leads to life, and those who find it are few.[53]

From time to time, it does us good to think on these things. There is a day coming that will sort the wheat from the chaff, the godly from the ungodly.

Thought

Read Prov. 24:11,12. Ignorance is unjustified.

Prayer

Dear Lord, open my eyes to see the lostness of the lost. Grant me your compassion for them.

---

[53] Matt.7:13,14

DAY TWENTY-TWO

Ps.1:6 (ESV)

...for the LORD knows the way of the righteous, but the way of the wicked will perish.

Our choices will determine our future. God sets before us the choice of life and death, and he strongly encourages us to choose life. We can walk the way of this world, imbibing its corrupted values and changeable wisdom, or we can walk the way of God, with its own distinctive values and eternal wisdom. I say eternal, because the wisdom of this world is constantly adapting itself to current circumstances and cultures, and is constantly rewriting itself as things change. The wisdom of God, on the other hand, is changeless and ageless. The apostle Paul talks of the wisdom of God that "is not a wisdom of this age" and also which had been "decreed before the ages" (1.Cor.2:6,7)

In verse 6, the song declares that the Lord "knows the way of the righteous". Matthew Henry wrote:

> *...he chose them into it, inclined them to choose it, leads and guides them in it, and orders all their steps.*[54]

This 'knowing' is a deep and intimate knowing – a careful and attentive knowing. It's walking under the eye, under the hand and under the care of God. Never are we out of his sight or mind.

It is vastly different with the ungodly. It is as if God chooses not to notice them, or the way in which they walk. Their life-constructs are ignored by God. They have rejected his counsel, love and wisdom, and so he lets them get on with it. They have made their choice, and therefore have no grounds for complaint when God takes no notice of their mishaps, nor does he step in to deliver them. Their way is trackless, meaningless, void of purpose and direction, and is leading nowhere except to a cliff edge. The root meaning of the Hebrew word translated 'perish' means to 'wander off'. It gives a picture of a sheep that has wandered off from the flock and has exposed itself to possible fatal danger.

---

[54] Matthew Henry, *Henry's Commentary, Vol.2*, (London, Partridge & Oakley, 1849), p.105

We can choose either a life full of meaning and purpose, or a life void of meaning and purpose. We can choose a life that is built on the unchanging and life-transforming words of God, or choose a life that takes more notice of the 'culture noise' around us.

Thought

Choose well. Don't let the wind blow you away

Prayer

Father, help me to plunge my spiritual roots deep into your life-giving word, making me someone of substance and an example to others.

DAY TWENTY-THREE

This song tells us strongly that the words of God, when we give proper, loving and disciplined attention to them, will cause us to be strong, stable, fruitful and steadfast. It also warns us powerfully and strongly of the consequences of ignoring what God offers. Don't let the wind blow you away.

I want to begin to end these devotions by retelling a story. It is found in its original form in C.S. Lewis' book 'The Magician's Nephew'. In the book, set in the magical and wonderful world of Narnia, a young lad named Digory was sent on a quest to find an apple from a garden located in the Western Wild. After a long and hard adventure, he brought the apple back to Aslan, the lion king of Narnia, knowing that this apple had healing properties. Aslan knew that Digory was thinking of his seriously ill mother, but he told him to throw it into the soft mud by the riverbank. In the morning, to Digory's delight, in the place where the apple had been thrown stood a magnificent and sweet-smelling tree, full of apples.

Aslan told Digory to pluck an apple from the tree, and then returned him with the apple to the world of men. When he arrived home, he ran up the stairs, cored and pared the apple, and fed it to his ailing mother. That evening, he took the peelings and the core, and planted them at the bottom of the garden. The doctor came the next day and was amazed at her recovery.

From the remains of that Narnian apple sprang another magnificent tree, and it began to bear the most beautiful apples in the world. But somehow, deep inside, the Narnian tree never forgot its roots. There were some very strange days when the weather was warm and still, that it would start to rock violently, as if in a storm. Somehow, the tree had become aware of gales blowing in Narnia, and it had responded.

I remember being profoundly moved to tears as I read about that. The cry of my heart rose up to God, saying that I would love to be like that Narnian tree; although planted in the soil of earth, I would somehow pick up and respond to the movements of heaven. I believe that those who give serious and loving attention to the Word of God shall be like that tree: although living on the earth, deeply rooted in God and sensitive to the movements of heaven.

Thought

When was the last time you somehow sensed what was happening in heaven?

Prayer

Dear God, please make me more alert to what is happening around your throne. Teach me how to 'listen in' to your deliberations with your heavenly council.

DAY TWENTY-FOUR

Yesterday we considered the Narnian tree of C.S. Lewis. Many years later, according to the story, it blew down in a large storm. Digory, now a middle-aged professor, couldn't bear to have it cut into firewood, so he had it built into a wardrobe, the one made famous by Lewis' book 'The Lion, the Witch and the Wardrobe.' Lewis wrote of Digory:

> ...although he himself did not discover the magical properties of that wardrobe, someone else did. And that was the beginnings of all the comings and goings between Narnia and our world.[55]

The Bible that we hold in our hands is a perfect similitude of Lewis' wardrobe. As we enter through the door of its pages, pushing deeply through as we go, we will find ourselves tumbling into the wonderful world, not of Narnia, but of the kingdom of heaven. As we continue, we will discover a world that is invisible to the natural eye, and we will find the God of heaven speaking to us. His voice will penetrate to the deepest levels of our lives, and we will sense the values of that kingdom wanting to become ours. We will feel his thoughts pressing into ours, refreshing and restoring our broken and ill-informed perceptions.

We, too, like the Narnian tree, will begin to discern the movements of heaven, and our speaking shall become somewhat prophetic.

So, we have sat under the shade of the first tree, the first song, as we go through the gate into the field of psalms. We have heard its wisdom and have felt the gentle pulling of heaven upon our spirit. It now beckons us to look further. There are more trees, more songs to encounter. They, too, will teach us their wisdom. They will also teach us the vocabulary of prayer, of worship, of praise, of lament. It all lies before us.

Let Philip Yancey speak to us about this amazing field of psalms:

> Psalms, located in the exact centre of the Bible, gives us a comprehensive record of life with God through individually fashioned accounts of how the spiritual life works. I come to the psalms not primarily as a student wanting to acquire knowledge, but rather as a fellow pilgrim wanting to acquire relationship ... More than any other book in the Bible, Psalms

---

[55] C.S. Lewis, *The Magician's Nephew*, (Fontana, 1955), p.171

reveals what a heartfelt, soul-starved, single-minded relationship with God looks like.[56]

Thought

Each day, a volume of songs and prayers sits on your shelf, inviting you to enter and experience the world of the kingdom of heaven. Will you respond?

Prayer

Father God, touch my heart, draw me into your world through your Word, and make me somewhat prophetic in my conversation with others.

---

[56] Philip Yancey, *The Bible Jesus Read*, (Zondervan, Michigan, 1999), p.115

Other Books by Alan Hoare

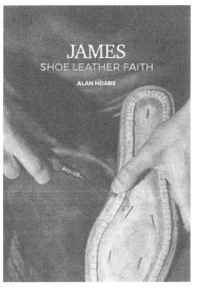

James: Shoe Leather Faith
ISBN: 978-1-78815-547-2

"The Scriptures must at times challenge what we believe and feel. The words of God not only heal and restore us, but they at times cut right into the core of our being, into the revealing of our hidden motives."

Alan Hoare's infectious enthusiasm for digging deeper into God's word is evident throughout this powerful 64-day devotional study of the letter of James.

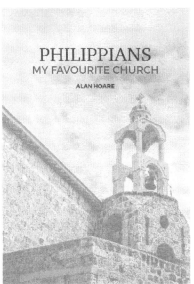

Philippians: My Favourite Church
ISBN: 978-1-78815-693-6

Through 100 daily readings, in-depth study and practical application, Alan Hoare takes us through Paul's letter to his "favourite church" – the church in Philippi. As he demonstrates how to systematically read and apply scripture, you will find yourself eager to start digging out the incredible riches and treasures found in the Word of God, not only on the surface, but also just underneath.

Available now from all good bookshops.

Printed in Great Britain
by Amazon

21861256R00034